ONE HUNDRED LIVES

LIFE & NATURE
POURED INTO POETRY

ONE HUNDRED LIVES

LIFE & NATURE
POURED INTO POETRY

D. A. JENNINGS

Editors:
Ted M. Zurinsky
Kate Lashley
David L. Jennings

ALSO BY D. A. JENNINGS

Seize the Cheese

American Sports Legends:
Your Turn to Score

Voices of the Susquehanna
Volume III
Poetry and Art (Contributing poet)

Available at *dajennings.com*

DEDICATION

Friend, encourager, prayer partner,
life teacher and mother
Nadine Jones
Happy 90th

Copyright © 2016 by D. A. Jennings
All rights reserved.

Inlet Shade Publishing

ISBN: 0-9966550-1-8
ISBN-13: 978-0-9966550-1-9

All rights reserved. No part of this book may be reproduced in any form or by any electronic or mechanical means, including information storage and retrieval systems, without permission in writing from the author, except by a reviewer who may quote brief passages in a review.

Contact: *dajennings@dajennings.com*

Book cover design by *Victoria Jennings*
Two images used under license from *Shutterstock.com*

PRINTED IN THE UNITED STATES OF AMERICA

Contents

Prologue
Life Beyond the Glass.. 1

Poems
The Inheritance.. 3
Where Buildings Compete for the Sky................. 4
Hero's Heart... 5
Pickers... 6
Bourbon Heat *(Southern Style)* 7
Photo: Young Woman Laughing........................... 8
Up in Smoke.. 9
Aging on the Interstate.. 10
Borrowed Secrets... 12
Barfly... 13
Wait for the Light... 14
Bottle of Tears.. 15
Photo: Don't I Have a Say?.................................. 16
Plastic Surgery Gone Wild................................... 17
Reciprocity Redefined... 18
Running on Empty No More............................... 19
Never Alone.. 20
Louisiana Sanctuary... 21
See What I Can't... 22
Everything Changes... 24

Highway Toll	25
Jackals	26
Photo: Sunnyside Up	28
Moving Beyond Today	29
Literary Porker Politicians	30
Once Upon a Full Moon	32
Alone	33
Knife in the Road	34
Beyond Science	35
CRASH	36
Magnolia Blossoms	37
Still Yourself	38
The Uninvited	39
Red Hat Rebel	40
Where Wisdom Resides	41
Busy Mom	42
Dinner in Darkness	43
Executive Duties	44
Charlie's Company	45
Waiting	46
Buried Dreams	47
Main Street	48
Photo: Morning Finds a Book	49
Stay Outside	50
Write Across the Page	52
Twilight's Aria	54
Wooden Promise	55
Winds of Lament	56
Please Don't Touch	57
Stepping into Morning	58

Snow's Forever Night...	59
Cell Mate...	60
You Will Treasure Me...	61
Wishes..	62
No Dessert Tonight..	64
What She Does...	66
Baby John...	67
After the "I Do's"	68
Photo: Wedding Bliss...	69
Quiet Pleasures..	70
First One Done...	71
Harry's Harried Situation.......................................	72
I Wait, She Smiles..	74
The Muse Whispers...	76
No Harm Done...	78
Boarding Pass..	79
While Angels Sleep..	80
Weathered Man...	81
Determined to be Stubborn..................................	82
The Crowning..	84
Restless Day...	85
Soul of My Shoes...	86
Life's Clock...	88
Faithful Friend...	90
Night Trade..	91
Write On..	92
Muscle Talk..	93
Robo Doc...	94
Percentages...	96
Photo: Strings of Dreams......................................	97

Slap on Smiles	98
Frequent Flyer	100
Time Bandit	101
Photo: Laughter Behind the Leaves	102
Butterfly Years	103
Call to Duty	104
Behind the Pen	107
Relationships Evolve	108
Flatulation Infatuation	110
Time Holds My Hand	112
Photo: Whoo Loves Ya?	113
Maestro's Touch	114
Hymns of Him	115
Central Park Wonder	116
Literary Escape	118
Wild No More	119
Secondary Rain	120
Eyes Now Open	121
Two Boys	122
Spending Time	124
Just Wait	126
Photo: Young Man on Steps	128
Unsold Canvases	129
Charging into the Heavenly Fray	130
People, Move Along	132
Imperfect Match	134
Only in America	135

Epilogue
Life Poured into Poetry.................................... 137

Acknowledgements………………..………………..……. 139

Notes………………………..………………………....…….. 140

Photo Credits………………..………………...…………… 141

Prologue

Life Beyond the Glass

Today I walked among one hundred lives.
Intrigue sauntered down the street on stiletto heels,
While misery pulled its heavy load through the gutters.

Through bustling city streets
Hope walked shoulder to shoulder with despair.
Ambitions hung on conversations at open-air bistros.

Tangled in the cacophony of everyday life
Laughter stitched the wounds of a previous night.
Cries heralded sounds of new birth and second chances.

Nature provided brief respites.
Solitary trails showcased earth's allure, and
God's mastery found expression in twilight's aria.

At day's end, I passed a storefront window.
Pausing, I reached forward and touched the glass.
A transparent life smiled back, and my hand pulled out
  a pen.

The Inheritance

Mama and Papa's house was never new.
It was born from scraps of splintered wood and rusty nails.
We kids fought to be king of the landfill, which grew steadily behind our yard.
Dented hubcaps shielded us from pipe swords pulled from abandoned buildings.

    Papa died two days after Mama.
    No one seemed to notice.
    Social workers never came.

Summer's glare still filters through dusty burlap curtains, made of stolen potato sacks from Smity's store.
Rooms within the house never stay empty.
Furniture is pulled out of junk-yards and forgotten neighborhoods.
Creaky bedsprings support third generation mattresses stained with other people's lives.

    No need to worry.
    We've got a house we call home.
    All us kids are doing just fine.

Where Buildings Compete for the Sky

    Thousand-dollar suits
    Walk above hundred dollar shoes,
    Yet can't stop to drop a dime in a cup.
Charitable hands are too often a scarcity.

    Tires screech, horns blare.
    Drivers swap barbaric gestures.
    Mouths sour into spurts of trash talk,
Motherly references fill the air with toxicity.

    Ritzy watches are offered for a pittance.
    Vendors peddle the latest designer purses,
    Priced to lure the gullible into their clutches.
Swindlers deal in mass-produced duplicity.

    Patches of material substitute for skirts,
    Stilettos and platforms hold their ground.
    Practiced smiles advertise timed pleasures.
Lipsticked ladies deal in epidermal electricity.

    Windows open up to red brick walls.
    Penthouses idle while owners vacation.
    Tenants wrestle rats for sleeping quarters.
Lifestyles burst with collective audacity.

Say hello to the big city.

Hero's Heart

Eyes, dark like black opal, hold the
Reflection of yesterday's flashes and flares.

Incoming mortars and sniper shots
Still echo through the chambers of his ears.

Aluminum wheels propel him to the parade,
Where flags wave and speeches are made.

Venders sell cotton candy and pretzels that seem
Flavored with gunpowder's lingering metallic taste.

Titanium and laminates move his silicon skin,
As he reaches up to place his hand over his chest.

Smiling, he feels the cool metal of his Purple Heart.
Beneath it, the life of a true American hero beats on.

Pickers

American Pickers excites viewers with what they tote.
Cotton pickers contribute to warm winter coats.
Nitpickers crawl under the skin and get your goat.
But nose pickers will never, ever get my vote.

    Watch for pickers who hide boogies from view.
    Under chairs and desks is where they're glued.

    Offer a tissue to those with nasal drip,
    With sleeves that snap like brittle chips.

    Avoid the ones who tunnel up their noses for food.
    Their dinning selections are revolting and crude.

    Move away from pickers who dig and flip.
    The projectile velocity stings like a whip.

On this subject, let's no more linger.
I've got to get rid of what's on my finger.

Bourbon Heat
(Southern Style)

Noon's air is fat with humidity.
Honeysuckle drips with the sweat of flies.
Mercury climbs the thermometer with smooth precision.
All else moves like a coon tick settling down for Sunday
    dinner.

Ladies of the evening,
Working the afternoon shift,
Wobble on open-toed stiletto heels
As glue releases its grip on their soles.

Mississippi River heat slugs over and around Jackson
    Square, and
Steams its way to burlesque clubs and luxury hotels of the
    French Quarter.
Creole cottages offer cool refreshment, while secrets stay
    tucked between sheets.
Only money separates professional ladies and the sizzle
    of a mid-afternoon dalliance.

Men wipe their brows with
Sweaty palms and damp kerchiefs,
Grinning like schoolboys ogling a centerfold,
Imagining things beyond their wallets and abilities.

Welcome, to Bourbon Street heat.

Up in Smoke

Smoke escapes from her chapped lips.
She texts cryptic comments into her cell.
Chipped nails tap the cold cement sidewalk.
She exhales.

Caressingly, the smoke surrounds her animated face,
Slowly sucking from it the firmness of youth.
She willingly invites the dragon into her lair.
With each breath he claims more of it for his dark den.

Coy and smiling, she indulges in youthful arrogance.
Believing that her body will never fail,
Her heart will never ache, and
The world will always revolve in her favor.

Stupid girl.

Aging on the Interstate

They don't fret about exceeding speed limits.
They're happy to drive less than five feet a minute.

Left lanes are their favorite place to slow down and drive.
With thousands of them on the road it's a miracle we
　survive.

　　　　　"Slowly count to ten."

Peeking over steering wheels, they motor along doing
　thirty-eight.
Not bad if they weren't tying up traffic on the interstate.

　　　　　"Take a deep breath and exhale."

Save your energy and words, they can't see or hear your
　gestures or shouts.
They're fixating on the road, trying to figure out
　what all the honking is about.

　　　　　*"Count your fingers,
　　　and make sure you haven't thrown any away."*

Why does their driving give us angst and white knuckles?
Because their experience predates seatbelt buckles.

> *Relax and give them plenty of space.*
> *In a few more years you too*
> *will be driving at a slower pace.*

Borrowed Secrets

Strangers tell me their secrets, but
Exchanged words never link us.

>I listen to their whispers.
I see every movement.
I learn about lives,
From the journals
On their faces.

Don't fault me for prying.
Intrusion is never my intent.

>It's the nature of a writer.
It's out of my control.
It's how I'm wired,
Because I need
To know.

>Rest assured,
Your secrets will be faithfully told.

Barfly

Over one hundred fifty thousand species of flies exist,
But there is one, not on any entomologist's list.
Known to fly at night, hanging with Bud and his brother Light, is
Barfly.

Three segments compose his existence.
Crowded rooms, mindless chatter and alcohol subsistence.
Dinner comes in liquid form; numbness from life is the desired norm.
Barfly.

Wings slow. Twenty to thirty days left to fly.
Scarred pancreas and liver present a tough way to die.
Initially, it went down smooth, now it's a life wasted on booze.
Barfly.

> No more, "Belly up to the bar."
> Fly.

Wait for the Light

Atop the bent bicycle frame,
Two skinny tires continue to spin.

Bystanders stare at the small crumpled boy, as
Sirens announce the arrival of the voluntary team.

Brakes screech and ambulance doors burst open.
EMTs descend, and kneel on the widening pool of blood.

A solitary finger searches for life on his tanned neck.
An ear is pressed upon his chest, listening for hope.

Hearts within the crowd beat in unified prayer.
Sobs from the driver beg for forgiveness.

A pinky finger twitches.
A soft moan is heard.

Racing to save his tomorrows,
They whisk him away.

Bottle of Tears

Time slows. It is not my friend.
Smeared red lips open and close
Like a snapping turtle.
Scorching words bellow, as
Hell's breath invades my nostrils.

Escape.
        I travel into my inner being.
                There are no needles.
                      No empty bottles.
                      Only soft embraces.
                No bruises.
        No marks.
No pain.

Time is immobile. It is nothing.
Silence brings me back to truth.
Oblivion is mother's release.
Using her empty bottle
I collect my tears.

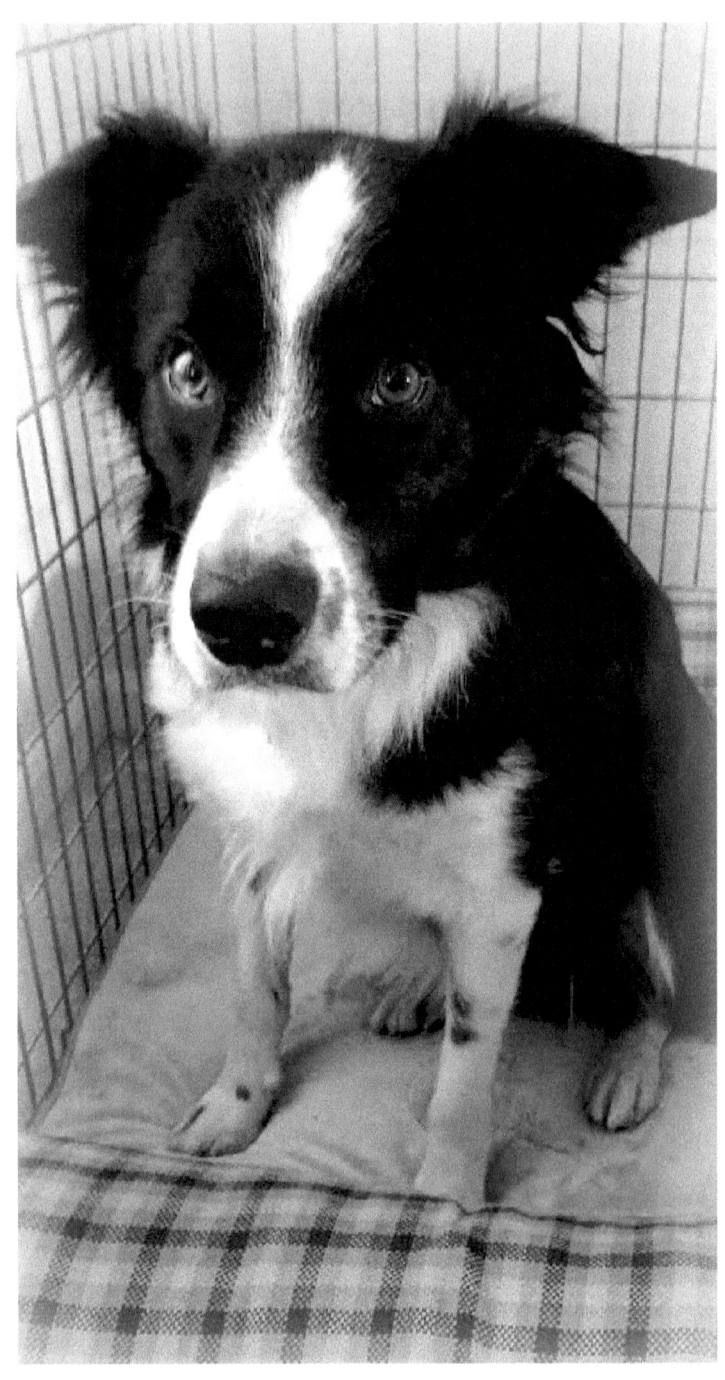

Plastic Surgery Gone Wild

Ounces of silicone or saline.
Can they elevate self-esteem?
Promote success or a better you?
It depends upon your point of view.

Women desire a bit more flair.
A trim here, bigger bumps there.
Men appear fit without hitting the gym, by
Having fat sucked out, to look younger and slim.

Confidence boosters are yours for a price.
And now your faithful pet can appear as nice,
Because technology has come up with a new device.

No longer does Fido need to hang his head in shame.
No more will he glare at you, since you're to blame.
Castration is now more "socially" acceptable,
Thanks to surgically implanted testicles.

Neuticles, the miracle invention of 1995
Will help Fido psychologically thrive.
Send today for your very own sample.
Perhaps your husband would want
  to set a good example?

Reciprocity Redefined

Share kindness, receive kindness.

                                                  An eye for an eye.

Give a kiss, get a kiss.

                                                  A tooth for a tooth.

Send a smile, catch a smile.

                                                  A life for a life.

                      Forgiveness for a cross.

Running on Empty No More

Leaning toward my sleeping ear
He whispers.
Waking to his closeness, I strain to understand.

Taking my cold hand
He weaves his fingers through mine.
Feeling his strength causes me to focus on my weakness.

With his free hand
He brushes away thin wayward strands of hair
From my hollow cheek.

Ignoring my cracked and shriveled lips
He places his upon mine
Sharing his kiss with me for the last time.

His breath floods my mind with memories,
Igniting snippets of time that fill my sails
Propelling my journey to the next shore.

Never Alone

Upon dew kissed grass I see your deadly traps.
Your lair waits behind the garden shed.
    You are there.
        Always you are there.

The sun reveals another hiding place in the spreading oak.
Your body shimmers with morning's moisture.
    You wait and watch,
        But never speak.

Into my room you creep when the splinter moon rises.
Your legs carry you noiselessly across the floor.
    You make your bed under mine,
        Waiting to steal my sanity.

In my dreams, my hands move in futile effort, while
Silken ropes bind my arms and feet, then my eyes.
    You will leave no prints.
        There will be no trace.

Solace finds no residence in my life.
Your mark cannot be exorcised.
    You will never set me free.
        Arachnophobes...
            Are never really alone.

Louisiana Sanctuary

Crawfish glide under the darkness
Of slime-green algae, and
Thrive within mud-brown water
Stained by rotting vegetation.

Forgotten memories creep
Over the stagnant liquid, and
Climb the banks, on the backs
Of gators and copperheads.

Fingers of history crawl between
Gnarled cypress and black willows.
Spanish moss sways at the touch
Of the dark, slithering spirits.

Midnight's mist patrols the muck and mire,
Hunting trespassers who disturb the souls of the
Choctaw and Cajuns, who found sanctuary here
Among reptiles, sawgrass and black widows.

Night is ending.
Dawn is approaching.
Secrets of the past retreat
Into Louisiana's muddy waters.

See What I Can't

Within the circular chamber I lie, with
A rubber life-line in my hand.
There is light, but I choose the dark
And close my eyes.

Cool air flows constantly around my face.
Tape binds my feet together.
An internal drum steadies my heart.

    Breathe.
    Focus.
    Relax.

Hollow, sporadic knocking begins.
Sirens come in three blasts,
Blaring and brash.

    Breathe.
    Focus.
    Relax.

Wood-peckers start their "rat-ta-tat,"
On hard imaginary trees, while
Jackhammers jolt the air.

    Breathe.
    Focus.
    Relax.

In my mind, Soldiers fire guns in bursts.
A faceless voice marks time passing,
"Three minutes. Good. Three more."

    Breathe.
    Focus.
    Relax.

Fictional gangs sound off with automatic guns.
Heavy metal bands pound out their beats.
Phantom bees buzz relentlessly.

    Breathe.
    Focus.
    Relax.

Torrents of noise subside with a final knock.
A rushing sound flows through my head.
I pull the yellow plugs from my ears.

Outside the circular chamber I stand, and
Exchange blue scrubs for my clothes.
There is temporary darkness in the unknown,
But I choose light, while waiting for the results.

Everything Changes

In that instant:

> Song birds harness their melodies and listen.
> Winds restrain the clouds, and both wait and watch.

In that flash:

> Screams transform into vapor and disappear.
> Pain is rebuffed, and replaced with irrepressible joy.

In that second:

> Unrestrained crying electrifies the air, as
> Tiny fists and feet punch out in freedom.

In that moment:

> Life takes on a new perspective and purpose, and
> Hearts are linked for the remainder of time.

Highway Toll

Rubber tires hug the asphalt along Highway 54,
   And the rain sets the beat for country station 96.3.
Rubber wipers favor a different tempo,
   As the trucker sings off-key to the road.

Empty plastic bags make their last stop on Texas cactus,
   And the wind whips them into a frenzied dance.
Empty coffee cups litter the floor of the semi,
   As the trucker fights sleep with another swig.

More cloud-covered miles are ahead, than behind,
   And the sun peaks out just before going down.
More deadlines keep his foot pressed on the gas,
   As the trucker passes another dreary motel.

Every truck plaza and petrol center holds a familiar face,
   And the moon shines on the empty seat by his side.
Every road owns him, until it releases him to come home,
   As a child grows up, and a wife grows old.

Jackals

Purple strands spring from the roots of her jet black hair.
Shaggy bangs hang low over hazel-green eyes.
For the moment, the street corner is serene.

Fifteen minutes pass. Then, they gather like jackals.
Conversations abound, but no words are directed to her,
Only questioning, judgmental stares.

Ringing cell phones prick her nerves, as she watches
  thumbs nimbly respond.
One boy slowly moves around her, capturing her anxiety
  on his camera.
Self-consciously, she bites her top lip; her breathing
  becomes erratic and fast.

Two bottle-blondes give her disapproving frowns, then
  exchange whispers and laugh in unison.
One pulls her guy closer, and marks her property by
  licking his cheek; one flicks her hair and turns away.
Their clothes are American Eagle, Abercrombie and
  Fitch; hers are definitely not.

Like carnivores hunting prey, they surround her.
Personal space evaporates as they slink forward.
She would run, but there are no openings for escape.

From down the block comes the diesel's thrum.
Someone tugs at her hair, as a precursor for tomorrow.
Quickly, the pack assembles into a single line.

Now she sits,
alone among jackals
on a crowded yellow bus.

Moving Beyond Today

Broken under the crush of life
My limbs give way, and
I find myself
On my knees
In the garden.

Ants march before me, fueled with
Energy pumped by tiny hearts.
Earthworms slowly plow.
Spiders construct
Food traps.

Squirrels scamper from oak
To hickory to soft pine.
Wrens and warblers
Chat overhead.
A dog barks.

Warm breezes
Drag clouds away.
I get off my knees,
And stand firmly
In the garden.

Literary Porker Politicians

Citizen, be alert and ask,
"For whom the fat rolls?"
Nation, stay watchful
Against the whims of hog bondage.

> This is no country for old choppers, or those
> Who waste and drink nectar in a swill.
> Pale kings and porkers awake!
>
> Have we created a monstrous regiment of sows?
> Is this a country where piglets fear to tread?
> What lies on the other side of pork, or this side
>   of bacon?
>
> Pray tell, what are the paths of pigs?
> Must we accept farrowing a time of graft?
> How far can money travel on the wings of
>   the pig?
>
> Do we face the same fate of gilt and men?
> Envision the horrors when the pink pigs laugh.
> How sleep the porker politicians?"

Look homeward, pigs.
Oh bacon, be not proud!
See clearly the house of fat.

Be gone with the swill!
Stand and salute a farewell to fat.
Do not be part of a confederacy of swine.

At least I tried.
I see the truth now.
I know why the caged porker sings.
His stablemate is the trendy cash cow.

Once Upon a Full Moon

Clouds snake around the full moon, while
Zombies drag their feet down sidewalks, with
Outstretched arms and three-worded chants of warning.

Capes flutter above evening breezes, as
Super heroes patrol neighborhoods, and protect
Foraging children, leashed pets and wandering parents.

Stormtroopers wield blaster rifles in search of
Red-lipped clowns with big feet and
Decaying smiles.

Witches weave their way through cloaked vampires,
To be first to examine the sweet provisions that
Send chills down the backs of dentists.

Freckles and bangs cover the face of the cowgirl,
Who stands side-by-side with pirates,
Gibbering minions and ghouls.

>   Hallow is the night
>   When all creatures coexist.

Alone

Tonight
I find myself
alone.

I'm glad
I do.

Because
that means
you're gone.

Knife in the Road

There is no fork in my road, but instead a knife,
It's Damocles' sword over my life.
Trembling and wavering I stand in fear,
Knowing too well what brought me here.

Circumstances cannot be erased,
But there are ways to leave no trace.
Can morning's light make things clearer?
Will I be able to face myself in the mirror?

Am I looking to save others from sorrow, or
Does my choice only concern my tomorrow?
Tell me now, the night is nigh,
Does an unborn soul really cry?

Beyond Science

Observation

Hearts rhythmically propel life.
They are blessed, broken and followed.
Some are stolen, poured out, or worn on sleeves.

Academia

Research and science debunk this organ's
Cadenced hold on life's emotions and decisions,
Claiming reason and doubt do not find sanctuary here.

Questions

Can it be denied that life is perpetuated with each
    pulsating beat?
Does the soft, steady murmuring not serve as the first
    lullaby?

Hypothesis

Brains may host scientific facts and
Opportunities to apply it with wisdom, but
Humanity is inherited through the beating heart.

CRASH

Sleep sidesteps night's grasp again, as
Fatigue kidnaps muscles into submission.
Cactus spines prick tightened blood vessels.

Nerve endings are frayed with desire.

Zombies wait in crooked lines for shots of soothing warmth.
Hands tremble for the elixir that gives clarity to life and satisfaction.

Gladly they hand over their money.

Depression and anxiety evaporate in the presence of its effect.
Life is again manageable, and all is right with the universe.

Cravings are gratified.

Coffee cups are soon discarded.
Clear-eyed workers scatter to waiting offices.
Energy abounds ... until caffeine fades into night.

Magnolia Blossoms

Along the languid Mississippi River,
Where southern waters run with the blood
Of brave soldiers from both North and South,
Grant's anaconda tightens its grip on Pemberton.

Vicksburg surrenders its fortress and final breath.
Cries of mommas, wives and sisters reach heaven,
As husbands and sons lay wounded and dying
Under waxy leaves and sweet blossoms.

                Momma planted a sapling.
                She watered it with tears.

                              Nothin' civil about civil war.
                              Nothin' casual about casualties.
                    One day, not soon, but one day, her
Magnolia will blossom, but it won't forget its roots.

Still Yourself

Shhh.
Seize time.
Silence noise.
Suspend motion.

Take on injustice.
Tap happiness.
Tame anger.
Taste life.

Invent.
Improve.
Impart love.
Ignore gossip.

Labor truthfully.
Limit spending.
Laugh daily.
Listen.

Learn.
Lead bravely.
List each blessing.
Live beyond yourself.

The Uninvited

Violence invites itself to the neighborhood, where
Warm whiskey loosens hot tongues, and
Night's cover exposes dark hearts.

Jaws misalign on impact of adrenalin-filled knuckles.
Bones snap under the force of makeshift weapons.
Bystanders seek refuge behind cars and prayers.

Profanity bleeds out into moans.
Sirens scatter the ambulatory into alleys.
Flashing lights throw staggering shadows against houses.

> In the end, all leave.
> Some in cuffs, some on gurneys.
> A few are bagged after exhaling their final breath, then
> Zippers close their teeth indiscriminately over
> Vipers and lambs.

Red Hat Rebel

Decades of propriety
Fill each crevice of her past.
Matching hats, gloves, shoes and purses
Line her closet and fill the chiffonier and armoire.

Post, Crocker and Heloise
Hold center stage on her bookshelf.
Walls are peppered with baby bums and
Toothless grins, grand weddings and grandchildren.

The family bible remains open on the coffee table.
Verses that have comforted, are underlined.
Supplication and thanks fill the margins.
Bookmarks plump up pages.

                    Yesterdays are
              Good, solid, predictable.

                      Today is
              Giddy, scary, petrifying.

                                She slips on a purple blouse.
                        A red hat waits for her impatiently.
                    Hesitantly she puts it atop her gray hair.
                Her heart races as she views the clashing colors.
          With a rebel's spirit, she heads out for her first luncheon.

Where Wisdom Resides

Grass glistens with dawn's dew.
Rays reach out to illuminate first light's nectar,
Giving the sun strength to lift itself into the sky
Where it dances with pink clouds from yesterday's
  dreams.

Birds busy themselves foraging food.
Worms find refuge from the damp earth, by
Prostrating themselves against the cool concrete.
Unknowingly, they advertise themselves as today's
  breakfast.

Animals angle for dominant domain.
Territory is marked, lips curl, teeth are barred.
Guttural growls and menacing eyes triumph,
Claiming the choicest trash from the smelly heap.

> At the vibration of success,
> The eight-legged wonder labors.
> Storage bags are knitted, and then
> Quietly and patiently he waits again.
>
> Beyond the reasoning of man,
> Nature nurtures my seeking soul, for
> Wisdom resides on the spider's thread.

Busy Mom

Stroller's packed and ready for mom's morning jog.
Under baby's arm is tucked a plush green frog.

Three sweaty miles and it's time for a shower.
Need to make it fast, his play date's in an hour.

Now buckle up baby and off to the store.
Diapers and milk...oh no, he spit up on the floor.

Bags are in the house; baby's back in his seat.
Late to church to discuss the winter retreat.

Roll into the parking lot, roll out the stroller.
Smell the aroma of fries, and burgers in the broiler.

Zip home, watch the news and get dinner ready.
Put baby in the swing with a soft brown teddy.

Table's set, hubby's home.
Baby cries, reach for the phone.

Grab a bottle, place him in the crib.
Enjoy a restful moment, now change his bib.

Dishes are done, after a busy day.
Get some sleep for tomorrow's relay.

Dinner in Darkness

Weak eyes scan the darkness
    aching for a shadow, a silhouette.
Hands touch what they cannot see, and
    ears lay dormant within stillness.

Approaching footsteps echo
    on worn stone.
A metal key disturbs rust
    inside the lock.

Words are not uttered, as hardened sulfur
    scrapes across rough wood.
Seductively, the burnt wick
    beckons the fire's kiss.
A hesitant flame wrestles gravity
    as it descends into the glass jar.

Faint acrid smells mesh into the
    scent of boiled potatoes.
Light plays upon the dark liquid and
    corrals demons into the bowl.
The growing hot wax mocks the life of
    the single trembling flame.

                Food is but a brief reprieve, but
                perhaps it is more than I deserve.

Executive Duties

Men and women are hired and join the cadre.
Mission statements are given and rallied.
An executive's vision is passed on.
    Department goals are relayed.

Pinstripe suits discuss intern dossiers.
Profits and losses are scrutinized.
Executive decisions are given.
    Assignments are made.

Stockholders and investors enjoy a free buffet.
Shares and strategies are hyped and touted.
An executive speech is delivered.
    Risks and profits are weighed.

Tired custodians remain to prepare for the next day.
Trash cans are emptied; vacuums begin to hum.
An executive leaves, calling each by name.
    Respect is shown this way.

Charlie's Company

Vietnam vets ride the asphalt on 83.
White hair. White beards.
Straddled on Harleys.
Outpacing echoes
Of bullets, and
Shadows.

Battalion insignias stitched on leather.
Black vests. Black jackets.
Weather beaten hands.
Engines roar above
Protests from
The past.

Vietnam vets ride the highways.
Red blooded. Red hearted.
Straddled on Harleys.
Racing to come
Home, at
Last.

Waiting

Opportunity doesn't come knocking for the graduate.
Employment stops before getting to his door.
...So he waits for motivation.

Permission to proceed is withheld by parents.
Approval sidesteps her attempts to please.
...So she waits for courage.

Companionship is thwarted by his shyness.
Love is someone else's happy ending.
...So he watches TV.

Family and friends aren't perfect.
Feelings are exposed and raw.
...So you wait to forgive.

Wait no more.

Buried Dreams

Rusty tractors and rotted wood lay forgotten
Under tangled ragweed and creeping vines.
Parched earth entombs yesterday's salt from papa's sweat,
Yet birds chirp and lay eggs in hollows of dead engines.

    He lived in a different time.
        He was a stubborn man.
            He loved one woman.
                He owed no one.

Today Papa was buried next to Mama.
Dirt covered dreams, which his children didn't share.
Tomorrow new machines will roam this land,
Making way for other men with different plans.

Main Street

In darkness I wait silently for your arrival.
   Morning's kiss illuminates softwood floors.
   An eclectic gathering of temporary residents waits with me:
  Paupers, murderers, priests, athletes, derelicts, lovers,
     noblemen.

                                 Make no judgments.
                                All are welcome here.
                                       Find me.

The sky above is held aloft by painted blue tin.
   Memories loiter of drugs freely sold within these walls
     Laughter lingers and pushes against the metal framed door.
   But a jungle, a bay, nooks and webs create a faceless
     chasm.

                             Progress disrespects dreams.
                             Futures become uncertain.
                                       Find us.

Soft ticking pushes time around a never ending circle.
   Empty chairs anticipate your presence and warmth.
   Piano notes long to travel through your beating heart.
   Inked pages endure night's cold waiting for company.

Yet fists tighten around the green.
Doors may close for the last time.
Find them.

Let your fingers run down each spine.
   Taste the sweet sensory experience of being.
   Breathe in the richness of paper, leather and ink.
   Free the prisoner within; step away from your cell.

If you want me to be more than a memory,
Find yourself, on Main Street.

Stay Outside

Winter waits outside the wooden house,
Armed with arctic blasts.
Bitter winds assemble,
And pound through
Cracks, toward
Annaleigh,
Who sits braced against the door inside.

Her children sleep nestled in innocence,
As spirits
Gather and
Flames dance.
Shadows flicker
Across their faces.
Dreams shield them from the storm's angst.

Trees groan under the weight of age and ice.
Limbs snap.
A branch falls,
Like a small child
Plummeting to earth.
Sound is silenced by snow.
Tonight's storm will quiet the voice of one more.

No other has the burden of Annaleigh's cross.
Others enjoy life and tomorrows,
Ignorant of her sacrifices.
Preceding blizzards
Still sting her with
Unforgotten losses,
And yet they return demanding one more.

Gladly would she welcome the forever sleep of snow.
But who else would make such damning choices?
Submission embraces Annaleigh; she casts lots.
She strokes his soft cheek, the child stirs.
Bare little feet reach for the floor.
No slippers await.

Hand-in-hand they approach the door and lift the
latch. Responsibility and resignation
Haunt Annaleigh.
Eyes that trust,
Blink in fear,
But he obeys
Her whisper to go...stay outside.

                                              The offering is accepted.
                                                The blizzard subsides.

Write Across the Page

Gather words.
Seize their power.
Write across the page.

Strike them.
Change them.
Give them life.

You're the master,
Until the last period.
Print, pray, send, wait.

> Typed words lay mute within the manuscript,
> Hoping to find appreciation and an audience.
> But like old whores, they pass time without
>   purpose,
> Waiting for customers who never materialize.

You're the slave,
Haunted by rejection.
Breathe, regroup, move on.

Strike back.
Never relinquish.
Rouse yourself for battle.

Gather new words.
Rejuvenate your pen.
Script honestly and boldly.

>Fling your thoughts across the page.
>Taste the stories that scream to be told.
>Rework, reinvent and revitalize the old whore.
>Let the story earn a dollar on the street.

There's no choice,
You're a writer.
So write.

Twilight's Aria

As the sun gradually collects its rays and
    begins the journey to tomorrow's dawn,
Twilight begins to sing a lullaby to the
    darkening sky amid waking stars.

The aria gently echoes between stoic mountains,
    and skims the ocean's white peaked waves.
Melodic notes urge sunflowers to surrender
    their brilliant color to the oncoming night.

Soft breezes carry lyrical whispers through
    boughs of aging trees and fields of wildflowers,
Calming playful leaves, deer and foraging fox
    among blankets of thistle and grass.

Twilight's song flows with the winding brooks
    so they may hear the caress of night,
Which quietly pulses with the rolling rhythm
    of the bullfrog's deep throated refrain.

Moonlight scatters jewels over ponds and rivers
    and watches them shimmer at this moment,
When twilight's aria connects the delicate thread
    between day and night.

Wooden Promise

Lopsided hearts carved into an old tree
link names together, but not lives.

Seasons fall prey to storms.
Roots, once strong, wither.

Torrents of wasted tears
and erratic heartbeats
prohibit peace from entering
my fortress of bitterness.

My next heart will be fashioned
from rocks and mortar.
All attempts to enter
will be rebuffed.

Sandman hushes
the wooden promise of
"happily ever after"
and allows me to dream.

Winds of Lament

A nor'easter bellows in disdain.
Lifeless trees nod in empathy.
There are none to fight over what remains.
No voices exist to offer sympathy.

Easterly winds search for selflessness,
Seeking any who would take heed.
But none survived the sword of selfishness.
Earth's gifts have been overtaken by greed.

Gone are the fields of blooming aster.
Melodies ache for choruses of birds.
Man has ordained his own disaster,
Destroying all fish, fowl and herds.

One was the culprit of such wrath.
Each person wanting one more of this, one more of that,
Ignoring intimations along life's path,
Failing to calculate loss, under exponential math.

Who witnesses the wind's strength and power?
Who tarries to rest in the bosom of the setting sun?
Who dances upon fields of flowers?
Winds lament, "No one. Yes, not one."

Please Don't Touch

Today a kiosk vendor grabs my hand in one motion,
Slathers it with a creamy-white coconut lotion,
Promising, "It's the best wrinkle-free potion."

A bored, mall hairdresser spots my uneasy state,
Gives the nod that she can relate. Then her eyes elevate.
Running over, she fingers my hair and declares,
  "It's too dry, too straight."

A matronly woman soon exits a store, and runs at me
  full throttle.
Embracing my stomach, she exclaims, "You'd make a
  great maternity model!"
"By the way, have you decided to nurse, or do you plan to
  use the bottle?"

    Tummy touching,
        Hair handling, and
            Creamy caressing
                Turn my hand into a fist, and...

Before putting them all in their place, here comes a
  morbid twist.
Bolting from the scene I scream, when I see the
  approaching smile of my proctologist.

Stepping into Morning

Rays of the sun begin to
Peek through night's covering,
Revealing idle cars on silent streets.
Yesterday's dolls and bikes litter front lawns.

Parents in pajamas quietly open house doors to
Release eager paws scampering for grassy yards.
Sounds of the cricket's nighttime lullaby diminish
Under the raucous voice of the raven's blunt "kraaak."

A car motors through the neighborhood.
Growls and hums emerge from waking mowers.
Weedwackers whirl into motion slaying dewy grass, as
Children scurry through front doors to claim abandoned
   toys.

Saturday morning rituals have begun.

Snow's Forever Night

Snow, concocted in a dirty lab,
Falls on eager outstretched tongues.
Innocents fall prey to the white flakes, as
The white powder quickly multiplies.

Drifting in a crooked path,
Snow crystals tickle and stimulate noses.
Its magical allure beckons all ages.
Both genders revel in temporary escape.

Trade winds carry it from south to north, and
West to east to spread its flourishing power.
It gathers force, it deadens the senses.
It muffles the sound when heaven and earth collide.

Intricacies of each flake become lost among dilated eyes.
Now in control, the pallid cloak blocks out the world.
White fades to black as weary eyes close tight, and
Voices fade silently into snow's forever night.

Cell Mate

Get off your phone.
I'm sitting right here.
Give your attention
To the one that's near.

Turn it off, and tune me in,
We're on a date, those beeps will wait.
Be with me right here, right now...
    Our first dinner's not going so great.

Enough with those video games.
I'm not interested in winning streaks.
Who cares about high scores?
    No one warned me about techie geeks.

I've had enough.
Keep your gadgets and games.
I'll look for someone else, who
Can do more than tweet my name.

You Will Treasure Me

Yesterday you knew me not.
  Dew had not left the bud of your infancy.
    Thoughts of indestructibility awaited your youth.
      Promises of forever still listened for their cue.

Today I live in your shadow.
  You sense my presence, but do not ponder me.
    The luxury of present and future ambitions is yours.
      How ignorant you are; soon you will yearn for me.

Tomorrow, when you can no longer dance,
  I will dance for you.
    As time rips away all you value,
      I will wait for your summons.

Tomorrow you will turn to me, and
  Loved ones will live again to share your joys.
    Weathered songs will relive their refrains, and
      Youth's exhilaration will be yours once more.

When there are few tomorrows,
  You will call on me, and
    I will come, and
      You will treasure me.

Wishes

Circling the block again, I finally see
The elusive parking space waiting for me.
With signal on, the ritual parking maneuvers start,
When a VW bug comes from behind and zips in to park.

Man, I wish I had
a designated parking space
that would set me apart.

Theater lights signal intermission time between acts.
Females race to relive themselves, like wolves in a pack.
One minute to go, my bladder's at the point of no return.
When a child cuts me off, leaving my kidneys in a burn.

Man, I wish I had
a designated stall
so I wouldn't have to wait another turn!

Theme park lines snake slowly; I'm now two hours older,
And the water at the base of the ride is getting colder.
Then, with goal in sight, children lose their whines,
When a group of punks buck the line.

Man, I wish I had
a quick pass
to assert myself ahead of these swine.

Metal scrapes, cars flip, glass shatters.
Every inch of my body has been badly battered.
An official card now dangles from my car's mirror,
It possesses the power to put me ahead and get me nearer.

Man, I wish I had
made my wishes a littler clearer.

No Dessert Tonight

Telltale signs of creamy shrimp bisque
Disappear with a dainty touch of linen.
Light touches of thunder-red lip gloss
Transfer silently to the same napkin.

As a witness to the poetry of her graceful movements,
Nothing prepares me for the horrific skirmish to follow,
    when...

Tenderloin takes refuge between her first molar and
    second bicuspid.
The linen napkin, with which she is equipped, becomes
    useless.
Her tongue plunges into action under the protection of her
    upper lip.

Over central and lateral incisors, the red muscle flies
    unrestrained.
Rounding the bend, mucosa crawls over slimy canine
    enamel.
With accelerating speed, papillae are the first to reach the
    premolars.

Surely she will swallow her thrashing tongue and gag!
No. Yes. No. The frenum provides restraint, and
  saves the day!

The errant meat strand is captured and swallowed.
Her eyes swell with triumph and satisfaction.

Dignity returns with a dab of her napkin.
I request the check, before she can ask for dessert.

What She Does

For a Garden
Knockout roses thrive in her garden.
Hues of red, pink and yellow on soft petals.
Clippers tame growth and enhance their beauty.
    I see God's hands in what she does.

For a Child
Uncertainties diminish in her presence.
A small girl, in a strange country, finds a friend.
Bonds are created with a head band and a ring.
    I see God's smile in what she does.

For Animals
Abandoned pets find love in her home.
Rejection is replaced with acceptance.
Lives are now under caring protection.
    I see God's care in what she does.

For Others
Their fears, pain, and loss reside in her heart.
The forgotten and abused are remembered.
Tears streak her cheeks; anger pumps her blood.
    I see God's love in what she does.

Baby John

Rain falls on the aluminum roof of our trailer.
Momma takes baby John outside to meet God,
Just like she did with Becka, Sara, Billy Bob and me.

 We look on as she lifts him up to heaven.
 We listen as she prays upward through the drops.

Thunder booms with each of her words.
Lightning illuminates her outstretched arms, and
Winds whip her hair, causing it to dance around her face.

 Her eyes are blind to the storm.
 Her ears listen only for His blessing.

Three hallowed drops fall upon her moving lips.
Only then does she lower baby John to her bosom.
Tenderly she kisses his forehead, and whispers thanks.

 There is no minister, no preacher man.
 Baby John has been baptized by God.

After the "I Do's"

Once "I do's" have been said, and
Vows are sealed with a kiss,
You'll take the first steps
On the search for wedded bliss.

Oh, we pray for smooth and carefree roads, but
We've traveled that winding highway too, and
Ruts and dead end streets are always within view.
So, with lessons learned, we lift up three prayers for you.

May good thoughts fill each day
  When sleep eludes you, and work is coming untethered,
  When emotions are headed for stormy weather
  Keep in mind what brought you together.

May angels give you words of
  Support and praise to exchange anytime you please.
  Make corrections privately, after praying on your knees.
  Say "I love you" often, with an embrace and squeeze.

May today's "I do's" become part of your life as you
  Serve each other as confidant, lover and friend, and
  Serve as a Christian on whom others can depend.
  Serve God faithfully until your journey's end.

God has given you the desire of your hearts,
As evidenced by you exchanging vows today.
Henceforth, you will be truly blessed, if you
Ask God for guidance in all you think, do, and say.

Quiet Pleasures

Quietly, I lie in morning's darkness,
Drinking in whispers of creaking floors, and
Feeling the soft push of air from the overhead fan.

Quietly, I see slivers of light overcome stars.
Entering through closed windows, they come
To dance on my pillow and whisk away slumber.

Quietly, I rise to morning's comforting sounds.
Snoring that still abides on the other side of my bed,
Giggling from our children's room down the hallway.

Quietly, I respond to scratches at the back door.
Swiftly he runs out, and I invite the sun to
Drench me in the light of a new day.

First One Done

What was the hurry to leave your mother's womb?
Where she held you safe in your custom made cocoon?

Your clock ticked faster than anyone else your age.
Your entire life you were eager for the next stage.

School was over, you found a job, and got engaged.
Secretly flying off to Vegas left your mom enraged.

Your desire for a family soon grew by two.
Your children always darting about, just like you.

Watching you grow became a favorite pastime of mine.
Wistfully I prayed the Lord would give me more time.

But why did you always want to be the first one done?
Didn't you know? Parents should never outlive their son.

Harry's Harried Situation

Harry wanted Mary to marry him, but was too shy to ask.
Frank had to be frank with Harry, "Ask her yourself."
Jack said, "People don't know jack. Do what you want."

> *Well, Harry got himself into a harried situation.*
> *He asked a friend to ask for him.*

Mary was not merry about what Harry had done.
Faith explained that Harry lacked faith in himself.
Drew, Mary's baby brother, drew a wedding picture.

April declared, "April is a great month for a wedding."
Summer replied, "Summer is better." Mary got angry.
Grace suggested a grace period for cooling off.

Rose brought a rose to brighten Mary's spirits.
Daisy gave her a daisy. Mary threw the flowers away.
Brandy brought over brandy, which did not get trashed.

> *Hope held out no hope for a wedding.*
> *Destiny believed it was Harry and Mary's destiny.*

Grant advised Mary to grant Harry another chance.
Mark marked a date on the calendar for them to meet.
Victor predicted that Harry would come out the victor.

    Victor was right.

Mercedes drove Mary to church in a Mercedes.
Melody sang a melody as part of the ceremony.
Paige thought one page could hold this love story.

    Paige was wrong.

I Wait, She Smiles

Again we wait for her to come running out the front door,
With pigtails bouncing; a bandage covering another sore.
I tell mom she's a girl; we shouldn't pick her up any
   more.

My mom smiles.

Teachers pair me with that tardy girl, built like a broom.
Her thick brown bangs swish, as she skips into the room,
And she promises me again that she'll finish her part
   soon.

My teacher smiles.

In a tux, I arrive at her house with flowers for her wrist,
And one more time she's late, so with her parents I go sit.
Finally, she enters, curls framing her face quite nicely, I
   admit.

Her mom smiles.

Organ notes ascend, as she descends the stairs.
A striking girl with auburn, upswept hair.
We waited twenty minutes, but somehow I don't
 care.
                              The preacher smiles.

Years slip by, we are blessed with a daughter and son.
Her ponytail still flies, for again she's late and on the run.
How is it that waiting and watching for her has become
 fun?
                                    She smiles.

Sitting beside my bedside, she gently strokes my hand.
I gaze at her soft, gray hair, held back by a single band.
With no regrets, I close my eyes to wait for her smile
 in a distant land.

The Muse Whispers

Sitting among strangers
Reaching for words,
Suppressing anger,
I scribble.

Waiting for motivation,
Looking for a prompt,
Listening for a cue,
I cross out.

Typing about the present,
Drawing from the past,
Imagining the future,
I revise, yet again.

Driving myself relentlessly
Night after night down literary
One-way streets and unmarked roads
I finally succumb.

Stalled, and staring at a blank page, I
Reach for the mug of two-day old coffee.
Yesterday's failures slide down my throat
With the bitterness of the stale brown liquid.

One step from giving up, I place my fingers
One last time on the smooth, squared keys.
One muscle tugs upward on my lips.
One word appears as I hear
A whisper in my ear.

No Harm Done

Lips move and a tongue weaves deceit,
Lingering on a whisper, falling on an eager ear.
There's no cause for worries.
It's a harmless lie.

Tongues gather strength in number.
Whispering gains volume and power.
There's no cause for worries.
It's a harmless lie.

Words are passed along unrestrained.
Tongues choose to embellish each word.
There's no cause for worries.
It's a harmless lie.

Lips move and a tongue struggles to apologize.
Sorrowful whispers fall upon an open grave.
There's no cause for worries.
It's too late.

Boarding Pass

I stand before my own reflection
Looking out at the bustling tarmac.
The plane's silver belly yawns open.

Luggage travels up the incline
For journeys not yet experienced, and
With remnants of stories already made.

Methodically, suitcases are jerked,
Thrown, piled, pushed and jammed,
Testing the integrity of worn buckles.

A zippered case jackknifes off the ramp,
Spilling open to the screams of a woman,
As her crumpled panties escape with the wind.

Seeing my reflection silences my outburst.
Looking down and clutching my boarding pass,
I get in line with my amused traveling companions.

While Angels Sleep

Be still my tired child.
   Close your sleep-filled eyes.

Enjoy dreams of home, and
   Bountiful tables that await.

Worry not about future troubles, but
   Rest in the peace of this moment.

As the sun sets, let its warmth
   Provide a blanket against night's chill.

Release your fears, and let me listen
   For your soft breathing.

Every moment I will be watchful.
   I am pledged to your safety.

While my angel sleeps,
   The devil will not dance.

Weathered Man

Before you stands a weathered man, with
Thinning hair and shoulders bent, and
Furrowed skin and shaking hands.

    Dulling eyes remember her lips,
    Soft curls and scented skin
    In the back seat of his car.

    Muted notes still resonate with
    Sounds of her breathing and
    Rhythms from the radio.

    Weak veins carry memories of
    Walking back to the prom
    Under a sleepy moon.

Before you stands a weathered man, under
Layers of time from decades of living, and
Furrowed skin and shaking hands.

Determined to be Stubborn

Three babies
Transform her twenty-six-inch waist into a larger size,
But she keeps the smooth, rhythmic sway in her walk.

Three toddlers
Fill her days with tantrums and diapers,
But she always sings them to sleep with a lullaby.

Three middle school children
Show little gratitude for her choice of clothes or food,
But she transports them to school, sports, and church.

Three high school students
Grow too old to be seen with her or wave goodbye,
But she watches secretly, as they board the yellow bus.

Three young adults
Put gas in their cars and move out on their own,
But she smiles as they drive away, while hiding her tears.

Three adults
Follow jobs and dreams and mates,
But she writes and stays connected by phone.

Three mature adults
Realize they were raised by an extraordinary woman,
But she taught them mainly through the way she lived.

Three senior adults
Notice she's become a little grayer, a little shorter,
But her mischievous eyes and devilish smile are stubborn,
 and forever they will be.

The Crowning

Comb the curls upon my head.
Adorn them with a ring of daisies.
Let liquid pearls of aloe scent my skin.
Powder my cheeks with pink rose.

Clothe me in blue lace and taffeta.
Put away my shoes so my feet may run free.
Lay me down upon sheets of whitest satin.
Kiss me gently, should you desire.

Cover me in darkness,
So I may see the light, for
I have walked my final path and
Am ready for my crown.

Restless Day

    Walk.

Behind us rests the city,
Slumbering under a blanket of lights.

Before us dirt winds into a path
Upon which the silver moon reposes.

    Be still.

Hear the gentle brook ripple.
Taste the sweet grass beside the trail.
See the doe and fox among thistles and mint.

    Be still.

Hear the peeling bark of the sycamore.
Taste the honeysuckle's sweet nectar, and
Smell the earth as it labors to grant life to the future.

    Be still.

Behind us breathes the forest,
As we turn back to the concrete city.

Before us waits a restless day, because
Asphalt inches toward the dirt path.

    Run.

Soul of My Shoes

We stand as two-footed cattle in the moving darkness.
Sniffles, cries, and that damn intervening silence.
Empty spaces in our living coffin are filled
With the smell of fresh and dried urine.

Movement stops and doors retreat into the walls.
Sobs ricochet throughout the crowded transport.
Hairs on my neck try to pull me into retreat,
But the herd unwillingly presses forward.

Each step tramples color out of the sky
Until only gray and shades of gray remain.
Whispers, averted glances, and more madness
As palms of children are yanked from their heritage.

My name and memories are my only possessions.
I now wear another's smock and wooden clogs.
They walk with me through each vile step
Into the sights, sounds and smells of hell.

Months and years go by.
Or is it only a day?
I stop asking.

One night, I dream of a rose.
It's white and soft, and it comforts me.
Then droplets of blood ooze from its petals.
Tears wake me, but the rose's lingering aroma calms me.

Morning news comes promising showers and freedom.
My heart dares to hope for the first time in so long.
I will leave the trappings of this nightmare.
But first, they direct me to undress again.

In darkness I feel myself slipping away.
My hearing heightens above the din of screams.
I hear a man find his God, another curses his God.
I want to cry out and warn someone, but who will hear?

As blackness washes away the final hint of gray,
I give my soul to the shoes with which I came.
Someday they will tell my story.
Listen ... and remember me.

Life's...

Twelve
Finally, I am home.

Eleven o'clock
Others clothe and feed me.
Food is bland, sounds elude me.

Ten o'clock
Pain is my companion.
Grandchildren bring joy.

Nine o'clock
I bury family and friends.
Career days are behind me.

Eight o'clock
Walking is my exercise.
I have gained weight.

Seven o'clock
Jogging is more suitable for me.
I work too long and hard.

Six
I race through life.

...Clock

o'clock
I float and quietly wait.

    One o'clock
        Movement is forced.
            I experience pain, then relief.

        Two o'clock
           Crawling is expected.
           I am small and fragile.

           Three o'clock
               Walking allows exploration.
               I venture toward discoveries.

           Four o'clock
               Skipping shows coordination.
               My skin continues to stretch.

           Five o'clock
            Youth and health are mine.
           I am invincible.

    o'clock
Running brings satisfaction.

Faithful Friend

Spilling over the wired basket, they languish at my feet.
Crumpled papers marred with tears and scribble,
Which mock my effort to scream my loss.

Words elude my mind and jettison elsewhere,
Leaving behind years of picture-framed
Memories and vacant tomorrows.

Just know my friend,
I will remember
Forever.

Night Trade

Night's shadow
Demands daylight and warmth to be repealed.
Steps approach with my name on their heels.
~

Church bells lament the grave's refrain,
Hell's bedlam spews forth the same,
A knock at the gate heralds the name
of Death.

Priests, preachers and rabbis come into sight
With tongues twisted and tied by the night.
A faceless voice screams out their plight,
it's Death.

Man turns on man, not a soul can he trust.
Rifles and bullets explode into dust.
Nails pound out the call of greed and lust
for Death.

Into the room you escaped with me.
Yet when I add, the count is three.
So, who is it we cannot see?
Death.
~
Forgive me as I sit, the last one of two.
For I bartered with Death to take only you.

Write On

Tremble not under the blind man's sight, for
He extends his boney finger into darkness
Searching for his own elusive importance.
    His words come from vanity and fear.

Ignore expressions from disgruntled lips
Formed from the bile of poisonous envy
Seeking justification for personal failure.
    Her words ooze from hollow talent.

    Stand unashamedly upon mountains.
    Call together the hordes of stories within.
    Craft each one with care and determination.
    Your words bring drops of life upon the desert.

Write as one blessed by God to capture and create worlds.
Write with obsession and urgency to remember and tell.
Write until fingers burn and sweat drips upon your page.
    Write until the pen is pulled from your lifeless hand.

    Write.

Muscle Talk

Is he mesmerized by his own reflection curling dumbbells,
While watching his biceps and triceps relax and swell?

    Then you can say, "He's narcissistic."

Does he wear tank shirts that compress his chest,
While gleaming with oil so others are impressed?

    Then you can say, "He's vain."

Does he strut around the weight room looking down on
    smaller muscled guys,
While his inner abductors wrestle each other between his
    beefy thighs?
    Then you can say, "He's self-centered."

Can he bench press 300 pounds more than you weigh,
While making it seem as effortless as child's play?
    Then you can say, "He's egotistical."

When he goes to exit the building, pushing past you,
While others are watching to see what you'll do,
    Then you can say, "Hey, wait just a minute!
    Uh, let me get the door for you."

Robo Doc

Versace glasses perch upon her head.
Dryly she flips through my file.
Dragging a red fingernail over the words
She grimaces like I'm already dead.
> *There will be no good news today.*

Silently she leaves as the technician enters once more.
Long needles in, no supportive words out.
Then the tag team switches yet again
As efficient, somber, and sterile as before.
> *I must review my last will and testament.*

The upward force of the doc's left eyebrow
Sets in motion the etch-a-sketch wrinkles
That streak across her pasty-white forehead.
Hang tight, the bad news must be coming now.
> *Should I contact the funeral home this afternoon?*

Staccato questions escape her clinched teeth.
Each of my answers is met with a sigh or smirk.
Answers are scribbled illegibly on the form.
Nothing will come of this appointment, but grief.
> *Will I have time to say my goodbyes?*

Omnipotently she performs the final exam.
No concerned words, no comforting efforts.
Not even elevator music fills the air.
Hope for the future must be damned.
    With heart racing, life's memories begin to flash by.

As she adjusts her glasses, she retreats behind her desk,
Then sits and looks at me for the first time.
Leaning back in her chair, she inhales the air
From the room and from my chest.
    She's contemplating how to break the news.

With this in mind I begin to pray,
Only to be interrupted by her
Lifeless words,
"Your fine."

Percentages

Mustard stains her uniform, but
Her smile glows with visions of a car.
Nothing big. Just enough for her and a guitar.
If everyone tips 20 percent, she'll be in L.A. in a year.

Business slows, the economy tanks, but
She puts on a smile and works double shifts.
Everyone feels the pinch. Patience. Things change.
If the regulars tip 10 percent, it'll be three more years.

Doubt seeps into the months, then a stranger enters.
His smile radiates promises of escape and adventure.
Nothing risked, nothing gained. Just what she needs.
A baby is conceived; he leaves nothing more, and is gone.

Fatigue walks under her feet, and radiates up her spine.
She puts on a smile, works double shifts and weekends.
Nothing lasts forever. Patience. Things change.
She gives 100 percent of her love to her baby girl.

Words, attached to musical notes, dance on her lips.
Her smile begins to sing with her baby's song.
Nothing fancy. Just the simple truth.
L.A. sends a 50 percent advance.

She loads up the car with
Her baby and guitar
And drives.

Slap On Smiles

Step right up.
Have I got a product for you?
It's been around since faces,
But now, it's new and improved.

    Leave the smiling to us!

Buy a smile on a stick, or
Select one with adhesive.
Choose from various sizes
To ensure your face is cohesive.

    But wait, there's more!

Eight amazing options are offered,
Each guaranteed to relax facial tension.
All come with a money-back guarantee.
Purchase it now, don't wait for your pension.

    But wait, there's more.

Conceal a yawn with a smiley cover-up, or
Let your smile sparkle with bogus sincerity.
All this can be yours for a very low cost, but
Be advised, it's cheap, but it's not free.

    What more could there possibly be?

                  So hand over your dough, and
                      Slap on a smile, and then
                          I'll be 'a smiling too.

Frequent Flyer

Eyes ignore the pantomimes.
A steward's mouth moves, but
Ears no longer listen for instructions.

Sleep overtakes weariness.
A hoodie hides a young face.
His feet dangle above the floor.

Behind the roar of the engine, a father lingers.
Beyond the miles ahead, a mother eagerly waits.
Between the metal wings, a child's heart splinters.

Time Bandit

Hands on my watch wave goodbye in minutes and hours.
Resentment saturates my tongue as my stomach sours.
Sand is funneling to the bottom of my hour glass,
While dickering about a punctuality impasse.
Why don't our watches ever align?
Why is her schedule more
Important than mine?
Today it ends.
No amends.
Hear me
Affirm
The
New
Me.
New
Rules.
No delay.
I am important.
My time's valuable too.
No more bogus apologies,
Accepted for illogical chronologies.
I'm standing up and taking the doormat off my back.
No more absolution for self-centeredness or any smack.
TODAY I'M TAKING CONTROL OF MY TIME BACK!
I'll give her 30 minutes to get here, so I can let her know.

Butterfly Years

Reports, meetings and research quietly
Drift and wane into the void of nevermore.
In their place, I hold two delicate chrysalises.

    My heart focuses on my children,
    Souls on the cusp of sovereignty.

Time for sheltering and protecting is passing,
As their independence begins to emerge.
They wrestle between tentative steps and flight.

    My children are no longer children,
    But butterflies who dance unrestrained.

Soaring beneath the protection of the oak tree,
Time kisses their lips as my greatest legacy.
To my relief, and grief, they soar.

Call to Duty

Rise and shine.
Duty doesn't wait for the sun to rise.
Buckle up, grab your gear, and
Kiss those dreams goodbye.
   Now get those boots on the ground.

Revolutionary War
      Shouts for representation and personal rights
      Ring out from thirteen young colonies.
      Patriots unite against the coats of red
      Carrying borrowed weapons for new liberties.
        Now find boots and hit the ground.

Civil War
      Slide bayonets into scabbards, and
      Keep pistols and muskets at hand.
      Forget sovereignty, union, slave or free
      You've chosen where you stand.
        Now march those boots on the ground.

The Great War
      Submarine attacks pull us in.
      Our forces join the Triple Entente.
      Terrain has changed over the years, but
      Today we fight on the eastern front.
        Now run those boots on the ground.

World War II
    Super powers have aligned,
    Totalitarians and separatists are at war.
    "Never again" is obsolete, so
    Joe and Jane, what are you waiting for?
        Now put those boots on the ground.

Korean War
    Another region fights a civil war.
    People's Republic teams with the North.
    The U.N. sides with the South, and
    Another cold war's coming forth.
        Now walk those boots on the ground.

Vietnam
    Advisors, trainers, and Rangers
    Clear paths for units to pursue, but
    Tunnels, jungles, tactics and rain
    Demand more feet to come in the queue.
        Now move those boots on the ground.

Desert Storm
    Stealth fighters and Tomahawk missiles.
    New technology helps the U.S. thrive.
    Air attacks pummel targets for weeks.
    Marines and Army infantry arrive.
        Now tramp those boots on the ground.

Afghanistan
    Attacks on American soil compel us to fight.
    Bombs fall, troops move in a quiet surge.
    U.S. forces bolster and boost the Afghan army.
    Settle in, additional resources will soon converge.
        Now keep those boots on the ground.

Iraq
    Capture terrorists and neutralize their efforts
    Eliminate weapon of mass destruction sites.
    Saddam is toppled and power is up for grabs.
    Coalition forces face guerrilla-style fights.
        Now plant those boots on the ground.

Americans march on throughout time
Offering up their youth, hopes and dreams
For an elusive peace of liberty and freedom for all.
Consider our gains and their loss as their boots
    Now get those boots on the ground.

Behind the Pen

    Never stepping into the arena,
They write of the weakness of the gladiator.

    Never pursuing a dream,
They express annoyance for nonconformists.

    Never possessing a talent
They scorn innovative performances.

                                 Never taking a risk,
                                  They shield themselves,
                          Behind the point of the critic's pen.

Relationships Evolve

1870's
Stars ready themselves for slumber as the sun
Stretches out its hand to claim the morning dew.
Light frames his silhouette; warmth from his kiss
Carries with it the heavy, lingering scent of cologne.
The taste of berries and chocolate still dance on her tongue.
He says, "I will call upon you tomorrow."

1940's
Across the sea he travels, called to fight another war.
Letters come, sustaining love through days they cannot touch.
Fingers trace the curve of each word and every sentence.
Ribbons tie January through December's notes; the box is full.
He promises, "I will write again soon."

1960's
Dinner's getting cold; wax pools at the candle's base.
Concern fades when his voice reaches her from a pay phone.
War protestors block roads; a longer route will bring him home.
He says, "I'll be home later."

2000's
Harried jobs, busy lives; countless demands on time.
Grab a coffee, drop off kids, commute to work, eat junk.
He texts, "There soonest."

2010
Instant messages, Facebook, snapchat, twitter, emails & texts.
He sends, :)

Flatulation Infatuation

Walking among us,
Eluding detection,
They let go, and
It happens.

Released silently.
Initially undetected.
It permeates the room.
Like a yawn it circulates.

      Noses crinkle.
          Eyebrows rise.
              Throats constrict.

Acting innocent,
Pointing at others,
They feign innocence,
By producing a smug smile.

      Fruit?
         Beans?
            Vegetables?

Babies and bosses do it.
Lumberjacks and ladies do it.
Large and small do it.
You do it.

But heavens no,
Not I.

Time Holds My Hand

Today I walk a short path.
My feet yearn to take another step and then one more,
But time holds my hand.

> Life beckons along the crushed stone trail.
> Trees step back at each bend waving me forward.
> White and Green Ash arch the path permitting
> Sunlight to knit the lace upon which I walk.
>
> In the distance a dog barks incessantly
> At an intrusion, or perhaps an illusion.
> The rivulet's murmuring goes undetected,
> Until it shouts from the sun's wet reflection.
>
> Droplets break against rocks and merge
> Beneath the darkness of muddy water.
> Winding streams subdue water into whispers,
> Which flow alongside history's silent tracks.
>
> Rhythmic sounds beat overhead.
> Air pulses around my bare shoulders.
> Wings ascend higher; calmness returns.
> Wild azalea and evening primrose smile.

Plump firecrackers, dressed as dandelions,
Wait for afternoon's zephyr to ignite, and
Catapult them on their way.
Breezes prod leaves to wave goodbye.

Monarchs and grasshoppers have forgotten me.
Owl and prey continue their perpetual chase.
Moving waters leave me behind as the sun sets,
But my words will claim them in my memories.

Today I walk a short path.
My feet long to take another step and then one more,
But time holds my hand.

Maestro's Touch

Ebony and ivory rest side by side.
Reflections from the grand piano cabinet
Capture the child's attention and draw him closer.

   A pudgy finger ignites a sound, which
   Creates a resonance within his heart.

Untrained fingers delight in conflicting notes.
Disharmony's excitement captivates him, but
Performances improve with passing seasons.

   Maturing fingers control flowing melodies,
   Then jump into distinct marching notes.

Mature hands now play upon keys of spruce.
Sorrowful passages surrender to his touch.
Audiences clamor for another encore.

   Old fingers perform one last sound.
   Maestro's music strikes a final chord.

Hymns of Him

White flour puffs lightly into the air, and settles
On a flowered table cloth and speckled linoleum floor.
Nature listens at Grandma's open window to hear
      Her favorite baking song, "Amazing Grace."

Peaches, picked this morning, simmer and bubble
In sweet harmony in the old dented pot.
Her narrow kitchen amplifies her voice as
      She changes to "How Great Thou Art."

Pinches of sugar settle into strips of dough.
The hand-cranked timer sounds off.
A breeze spreads fragrant news of her success, and
      She ends with "Just a Closer Walk with Thee."

Central Park Wonder

Central Park hums to the rhythm of a Sunday afternoon.
Acrobats goad visitors to part with a twenty.
Vocalists sing passionately for college tuition.

Sculpted writers cast stoic gazes over "Literary Walk."
Onlookers tarry at the Columbus statue, as
A small miracle unfolds.

Black bangs crest her forehead like a wet mop.
Impish features belie her graceful movements.
A shear midriff exposes a tattoo adorning her belly.

Not restrained by her size-one press-on jeans, she
Bends and retrieves a violin from its case and closes it.

> *How odd.*
> *A closed case.*
> *Doesn't she want tips?*

She slides the bow across a small block of rosin, and
Tunes her instrument to the brighter side of "A."

Her eyes close, a thin smile emerges and she begins.
Aznavour's "Quiet Love" silences the crowd.
Notes carry her brilliance throughout the park.

> *How amazing.*
> *A miracle of music.*
> *Who is she?*

Violin and bow now rest; all present are speechless.
She picks up the closed case by the handle, turns and
Disappears into the shade of the elms.

Literary Escape

Smooth pulp fiction bound in a soft cover.
History lives again with the flip of a page.

Passages of consequence shimmer in highlights.
Forced intermissions take pause at bent corners.

        Sigh with published romance pressed to your chest.
        Slam the covers together before evil triumphs.

        Shed tears for those who die in your hands.
        Share victory with detectives and sheriffs.

        Sail with pirates; fly with aviators.
        Scare yourself with night tales.

        Absorb inked pages
        And escape.

Wild No More

Tiny shoulders slump
Under the burden of existence.
Vacant eyes belie internal yearnings.
Wild horses pound blood through his heart.

Sealed lips hold his spirit
Which no one cares to know.
Small ears shut out cruel taunts.
Wild lions roar loudly within his gut.

Garbage cans are his café.
Sidewalk puddles still his thirst.
Shoeless feet wander busy city streets.
Wild pigs fuel the hunger in his stomach.

Life's stench enters his nose
Thru a door that cannot be locked.
Downcast eyes avoid disgusted stares.
Wild kids beat and bruise his insipid skin.

Dark alleys offer solace and rest.
Under the shroud of invisibility, he crawls.
Horses settle. Lions reconcile. Pigs relax.
Wild angels claim the child whom no one misses.

Secondary Rain

Between the first slap of thunder and the emerging
   voice of the sparrow,
Secondary rain is born.
Fate grants a longer life to it than others of its kind
Who immediately quench nature's thirst or
   evaporate into tomorrow.

Earthworms plow damp earth
Unaware of life above, where droplets
Loiter temporarily aloft the White Oak and
Ride the cups of daffodils.

Clouds aimlessly cross the sky as rainbows wake
   from slumber
To admire themselves in lingering drops.
Zephyrs sway water globules, tipping them to their
   second descent.
Laced shadows extend their brief respite.

Then...
Secondary rain is gone.

Eyes Now Open

Clarity creeps into my waking moments, as
Remnants of slumber hold my eyes closed.
Fragments of shadows and half-truths intertwine,
Revealing life's tapestry of discarded promises.

   Shards of yesterday's warnings prick my thoughts:
   Lingering wisps of an unfamiliar perfume;
   Unbridled eagerness to escape on business trips;
   Missed birthdays filled with pledges of "next time."

     Breakfast paints itself with tight-lipped smiles.
     Lunch finds relief in separate offices.
     Dinner disappears behind laptops.
     Night ticks away in different rooms.

        Truth took root in my dreams.
        Now I sleep with my eyes open.

Two Boys

Without previous introductions, they share a bond,
Recognizable by the colors worn around their necks.

Hands extend for a ritualistic handshake, as their
Eyes scan each other for evidence of bravery and skill.

Neither carries his knife today.
No trouble is expected.

With basic greetings concluded, both examine the street.
Nothing grabs their attention, until she exits the store.

Gray haired. Vulnerable. Lots of packages.
Her frail hand clutches the old purse.

In silence, they move in trained unison.
She is flanked by two teenage boys.

One reaches for her parcels.
The other for her elbow.

Together they maneuver her down a lonely street.
At a dark wooden door, they help her climb the steps.

Using the door frame, she pulls herself inside, then turns.
With gratitude, she takes her bags from the gallant Scouts.

Spending Time

Rising at four,
He readies for work.
Coffee in a cup, a bagel with a schmear.
Riding the in-bound train are seasoned suits, and
    interns making their premier.

Oxfords, Derbys and Monk Straps
Hit the station floor, jockeying for position
Alongside heels of Coach, Bradshaw and Klein.
The business shuffle is in full throttle, because those who
    can't dance get left behind.

No time for lunch today.
He grabs a bite from a machine.
Back at his desk he checks the time once more.
Deadlines missed will get you fired, and then
    you're out the door.

For the fourth time this month,
He stays late and cancels his date.
Work follows him home in his attache´.
Gets up and does it again and again for better
    retirement pay.

Time's been spent.
    He's paid off the house.
        A gold watch adorns his wrist.
      But no one's there to
    Hold his hand or kiss,
Or simply co-exist.

Just Wait

Justice wears a mask.
Patiently, it waits.
Behind a façade of indifference,
Its eyes consume all that unfolds.

Youth try to silence internal demons with
electronic assaults over laptops and phones.
Parents live on the other side of their children's
closed bedroom doors.

Shady dealer's market their products
wearing glassy eyes and plastered smiles.
Onlookers ignore illegal trades by absorbing themselves
in their own mindless pursuits.

Babies bear scars of drunken tirades of
mothers, fathers, friends and strangers, while
neighbors close window blinds
and cry.

Evictions discard the aged and helpless and
toss their belongings and lives onto the streets.
Greedy pockets become fat
from other people's misery.

Too many churches sing hallelujahs and hosannas and
pass offering plates to sustain hollow religions.
The poor and down-trodden
are not welcomed there.

Murder, lies, rape, and theft multiply without restraint
through cities and suburbs,
small towns and country lanes.
Who steps forward to testify?

Justice wears a mask.
Patiently, it waits.
Judgment will come to good people,
who see the madness and choose not to act.

Unsold Canvases

Restless sleep is his nightly companion.
Stubble grows from his face, while his
Hands twitch with the art
Waiting to be freed from his mind.

Faces, on unsold canvases, watch him slumber
As his genius synthesizes screams and
Laughter into colors and shapes, and
Transforms nature into triangles and squares.

Evenings find him alone on city streets.
Potential customers, lost in conversation
Pass by, oblivious to the masterpieces that
Remain locked in his room.

Charging into the Heavenly Fray

News of your passing comes on autumn's breeze.
Gravel on the path falls silent as I stop.
Clothed in the darkening frock of knitted clouds,
The sky gently cries with me.

Tears fall among the birch, maple and oak.
Like glistening memories, they cling to fall's final days.
Leaves clothed in browns, greens, yellows and reds
Slowly nod in sorrow.

Nudged by the growing wind, the leaves come alive.
Crunching under my weight, they chat about
Your gentle nature, mischievous grin, and wry humor.
Trees stand as firm as your beliefs.

Winds magnify and lift up each thought and word.
Life's colors spin, forcing remembrances to blur.
Above the cacophony of sounds and swirling images
A single dove coos.

Dancing leaves encircle me, and
Like a phoenix I rise out of death's anguish.
East and west winds part the cloudy curtain.
A brilliant blue sky beckons.

From life's fading colors you soar,
Charging into the heavenly fray.
Then, through the rays of light,
He welcomes you home.

People, Move Along

Emotions are released on a hardwood floor.
Boots, ballet slippers, and bare feet dance.
Which genius created such playful fun?
Change your moves with each song.
Lights come on, it's closing time.
Now move along.

                    Twelve years attending mandatory school.
                         Classes, once drudgery, now missed.
                             Why did it all end so soon?
                                Carefree days are gone.
                                    Graduation is past.
                                    Now move along.

Crying and regrets fill the apartment.
People, once in love, now are not.
What happened to the smiles?
Who was right or wrong?
The divorce is final.
Now move along.

> Red and blue lights electrify the night.
> Vehicles, once in a hurry, now slow.
> Could it be a drug bust or crash?
> Police wave the curious on.
> The excitement's over.
> Now move along.

Children are grown, the mortgage is paid.
Alarm clocks, once useful, gather dust.
Who is that old, bent person?
Health sings its swan song.
Youth has taken flight.
Now move along.

> There's more to your story.
> Now move along.

Imperfect Match

Thoughts wrestle inside his head.
Flames embrace their bodies.
Screams never leave his lips.

He watches her with another.
He strikes one match.
He watches her with another.

Screams never leave his lips.
Flames embrace their bodies.
Thoughts wrestle inside his head.

Only in America

Walking through the lower valley I see him.
I pause under the canopy of the mesquite tree,
And stand camouflaged beneath its shadow.

Rubber sandals expose his cracked and callous feet.
A straw hat, stained by the sweat of many years,
Casts a silhouette on the sun-drenched earth.

Bent, he moves methodically between rows of beans.
Brutal summers have scorched his hands a burnt brown.
His skin bears wrinkles belonging to an older man.

In the distance, a solitary bell signals the end of work.
Slowly, he slings the bag of beans over his shoulder.
A faint smile illuminates his face, as he carries away his
   family's future in an American dream.

Epilogue
Life Poured into Poetry

    Poetry is the gathering of words
    Waiting to levitate from inked pages.
    Unashamedly, it pushes reality away and
    Pulls you into times and places unimagined.

Once there, memories stir that have been long forgotten.
Pulses quicken for a story that belongs to someone else.
Tears drop for soldiers who never lived, but yet they died.
Belly laughs erupt when slapstick tickles the mind, and
Glances shift to basement doors where boogiemen reside.

    Poetry is the espresso of the written word.
    The choicest words are coveted and brandished.
    Excesses are squeezed out so remaining words
    Can invade the mind faster than a caffeine rush.

Once there, the spacing of lines takes control,
As it causes hesitation ... breath and thought.
Carefully placed words and short sentences become
Catalysts for enlightenment, or vehicles of escape.

    Poetry is life
    One line at a time.
    Reading it nourishes the spirit.
    Ah, but writing poetry frees the soul.

Acknowledgements

Strangers, observed from a distance, have unknowingly inspired a great number of these poems. Moments of their lives have been gently handled, interpreted and told with honesty ... and a bit of literary license.

Selected instances, from friends and family, also live within this book. I hope you find my rendering of your stories accurate and enjoyable.

Gentle prodding, encouragement and marketing are critical elements for the completion and success of this book. So, kudos to Pat Adelhardt, my Marketing Director and longtime friend.

My three extraordinary editors: Ted M. Zurinsky, whose comments are always right on target and inspiring; Kate Lashley, a member of our writers' group, who provided insightful comments to many of these works; and David Jennings, who continues to keep me writing, reviews all my poems and handles the business aspect of publishing.

And, as always, the rest of my family whose inspiration and support never falters: my mother Nadine Jones, brother Rob, sister Bonnie, daughters Victoria and Lana, and son-in-law Rodrigo.

Notes

"Plastic Surgery Gone Wild"..page 17

    Rachael Rice was the inspiration for this poem. Her penchant for current events makes her a sought after walking buddy. Neuticles is one product I will not forget ... although it would be nice if I could.

"Main Street"..page 48

    Carolyn and Tom Kulog own and operate Betty's Books in Baker City Oregon. In 1979 they purchased the business from her mother Betty Kuhl. Betty's pioneering spirit is the source of inspiration for "Main Street."

Photo Credits

Young Woman Laughing..page 8
    Courtesy of *Bethany Seiter Photography*

Don't I Have a Say?...page 16
    Courtesy of *David L. Jennings Collection*

Sunnyside Up.. page 28
    Courtesy of *David L. Jennings Collection*

Morning Finds a Book...page 49
    Courtesy of *David L. Jennings Collection*

Wedding Bliss...page 69
    Courtesy of *Courtney Borowski Photography, LLC*

Strings of Dreams...page 97
    Courtesy of *Bethany Seiter Photography*

Laughter Behind the Leaves...............................page 102
    Courtesy of *David L. Jennings Collection*

Whoo Loves Ya?... page 113
    Courtesy of *David L. Jennings Collection*

Boy on a Step...page 128
    Courtesy of *Bethany Seiter Photography*

www.ingramcontent.com/pod-product-compliance
Lightning Source LLC
LaVergne TN
LVHW052254070426
835507LV00035B/2757